How To Stop Being A Narcissist For Men

Practical Steps on How to Stop Being Narcissistic For Men

John Annabel

Table of Contents

Chapter 1

The Mirror Effect

In our selfie-obsessed, celebrity-driven culture, the term "narcissism" is frequently used to describe someone who appears overly vain or full of themselves. However, in psychological terms, narcissism does not imply true self-love. People with narcissistic personality disorder (NPD) are more accurately described as being in love with an idealized, grandiose image of themselves. They adore their exaggerated sense of self since it keeps them from experiencing intense insecurity. However, maintaining their delusions of grandeur requires a significant amount of effort, which is where dysfunctional attitudes and behaviors come into play.

A narcissistic personality disorder is characterized by a pattern of self-centered, arrogant thinking and behavior, a lack of empathy and consideration for others, and an excessive need for admiration. Others frequently describe NPD sufferers as arrogant, manipulative, selfish, patronizing, and demanding. This way of thinking and behaving pervades every aspect of the narcissist's life, from work and friendships to family and romantic relationships.

People with narcissistic personality disorder are extremely resistant to changing their behavior, even if it causes them problems. They tend to shift the blame to others. Furthermore, they are extremely sensitive and respond negatively to even minor criticisms, disagreements, or perceived slights, which they interpret as personal attacks. To avoid the coldness and rages, those in the narcissist's life may find it easier to simply comply with their demands. However, by learning more about narcissistic personality disorder, you can identify narcissists in your life, defend yourself against their power plays, and set healthy boundaries.

Narcissist Personality Types

Narcissism comes in several forms:

Adaptive Narcissism
This is when a person with this disorder focuses on positive traits like self-sufficiency and confidence, which can be beneficial. They can help someone

set high goals at work, for example, or enjoy satisfying relationships without becoming overly reliant on a partner.

Maladaptive narcissism
On the other hand, it is marked by toxic characteristics such as entitlement and a willingness to exploit others. The following are examples of maladaptive narcissism:

Overt or grandiose narcissism
Overt narcissists are typically extroverted, but also uncooperative, selfish, and domineering. Their exaggerated self-image and high self-esteem make them confident and assertive. They are also more likely to overestimate their own emotional intelligence.

Covert or vulnerable narcissism
It is common to think of all narcissists as dominant and overwhelming in social situations. However, covert narcissists are introverts. They are very sensitive to criticism and have low self-esteem. They can be protective and passive-aggressive, but they are less likely to exaggerate their emotional abilities than overt narcissists.

Communal Narcissism
Communal narcissists often see themselves as altruistic and claim to care greatly about fairness. They present themselves to others as caring and selfless. Their actions, however, are motivated by a desire for social power and a sense of superiority or entitlement. As a result, their actions frequently contradict their beliefs.

Antagonistic narcissism
Antagonistic narcissists, as opposed to communal narcissists, approach social interactions with a high level of competition. They frequently exhibit zero-sum thinking, believing that every situation has a "loser" and "winner. This worldview leads to aggression and hostility. They may be quick to criticize others while being slow or unwilling to forgive.

Malignant narcissism
Malignant narcissism can be a more severe form of the personality disorder. In addition to the typical signs of narcissism, a malignant narcissist may be aggressive, paranoid, or sadistic, taking pleasure in the suffering of others. They tend to engage in antisocial behavior, disregarding the rights and safety of others.

Excessive sense of self-importance

Narcissism is distinguished by its sense of grandiosity. Grandiosity is a false sense of superiority that goes beyond arrogance or vanity. Those who are narcissistic feel that only other "special people" can truly understand them because they are so special. Furthermore, they are far superior to anything average or ordinary. They only want to associate and be linked with other high-status individuals, places, and things.

Narcissists believe they are superior to everyone else and expect to be recognized as such, even if they have done nothing to deserve it. They will frequently exaggerate or outright lie about their accomplishments and abilities. When they discuss work or relationships, all you hear is how much they contribute, how wonderful they are, and how fortunate the people in their lives are to have them. They are the undisputed stars, with everyone else playing a supporting role at best.

Illusions of grandeur

Since reality fails to support their grandiose view of themselves, narcissists inhabit a fantasy world propped up by distortion, self-deception, and magical thinking. They conjure up self-serving fantasies of limitless success, power, brilliance, attractiveness, and ideal love that make them feel special and in command. These fantasies shield them from feelings of inner desolation and shame, so facts and opinions that contradict them are ignored or rationalized away. Anything that threatens to burst the fantasy bubble is met with extreme evasion and even rage, so those around the narcissist must tread carefully to avoid their denial of reality.

Constant praise and admiration

A narcissist's sense of superiority is like a balloon that slowly deflates without a steady stream of applause and recognition to keep it inflated. An occasional compliment is insufficient. Narcissists require constant nourishment for their ego, so they surround themselves with people who are willing to satisfy their obsessive need for affirmation. These relationships are primarily one-sided. It's always about what the narcissist can do for the admirer, never the other way around. And if the admirer's attention and praise are interrupted or diminished, the narcissist considers it a betrayal.

Sense of entitlement
Narcissists expect to be treated well because they believe they are special.
They genuinely think they should be able to obtain whatever they desire.
They also think that everyone around them will automatically accommodate
all of their whims and desires. That is their only value. If you don't anticipate
and meet their every need, you're ineffective. And if someone have the
audacity to defy their will or "selfishly" request something in return, the
individual should be prepared for aggression, outrage, or a cold shoulder.

Exploits others without feeling guilty or ashamed
Narcissists never develop the ability to identify with the emotions of others
and put themselves in their shoes. In other words, they don't feel empathy. In
many ways, they see the people in their lives as objects that serve their
needs. As a result, they have no qualms about taking advantage of others to
achieve their own goals. Interpersonal exploitation can be malicious, but it is
also frequently unintentional. Narcissists simply do not consider how their
actions affect others. Even if you point it out, they will not fully understand.
They only understand their own needs.

Frequently disrespects, intimidates, bullies, or belittles others
Narcissists feel threatened whenever they meet someone who appears to
have something they don't, particularly those who are confident and popular.
They are also threatened by strangers and those who challenge them in any
way. Their defense mechanism is contempt. The only way to neutralize the
threat and boost their own sagging ego is to bring those people down. They
may do so in a patronizing or dismissive manner as if to show how little the
other person means to them. Alternatively, they may resort to insults, name-
calling, bullying, and threats in order to get the other person to back down.

Chapter 2

The Roots of Narcissism

Many people with narcissistic traits may have had painful experiences that caused them to focus on themselves. These people may have become selfish in order to deal with early life difficulties, such as absent parents or bullying at school. Nonetheless, certain individuals may never have experienced trauma in this form, remain unaware of their actions, and genuinely believe they are the main character in many of their interactions with others.

Clinical health psychology practice suggests that there is no single root cause of narcissism. However, several factors contribute to the development of narcissistic behavior, as we will discuss below.

Excessive Praise of Abilities Over Effort in Childhood
When someone is born smart, athletic, attractive, creative, or has something else going for them without much effort, adults around them tend to admire them greatly.

However, admiration without recommending effort does more harm than good. As a result, the child not only adopts a fixed mindset but also develops a narcissistic attitude of:

> - *Entitlement to opportunities without doing the work to earn them.*
> - *Overvaluing natural abilities while undervaluing hard work.*
> - *Looking down on others who aren't as talented as them.*
> - *A deep need for continuous unhealthy admiration of their abilities, as the adults did.*
> - *Perfectionism in an attempt to gain even more admiration*

For example, I know a girl who was far more intelligent than the rest of her siblings. She was also beautiful, creative, and charming, which she was aware of because many people complimented her on it.

Unfortunately, because her parents were content with her passing grades, she never worked hard enough to reach her full potential. Even worse, she enjoyed being referred to as a genius because she never studied much but still managed to get good grades. The more people admired her abilities, the more she wanted more, becoming more entitled and detached from reality.

By the time high school was over, she formed narcissistic traits that she barely could shake off until she became aware of how they had damaged her life around 6 years later. In a nutshell, if you overestimate a child's abilities, they are more likely to develop narcissism.

Unrealistic parental expectations.
Children raised by perfectionist parents are more likely to become perfectionists themselves. So, because their parents showed them love when they achieved the excellent results they desired, the child perpetuates the vicious cycle, believing that they can only expect and even demand admiration when they reach perfection.

However, this becomes problematic over time because:

- *They begin to believe that because they strive for perfection, they deserve praise and superiority.*
- *They begin to believe they are superior to others because of the effort they put in to achieve excellent results.*
- *They are also afraid of criticism and act as if they never make mistakes.*
- *To avoid being surrounded by "mediocrity," they only seek to be surrounded by other people they deem successful.*

As you can see, all of these are projections of narcissistic personality disorder.
When you dig deeper, you'll discover that they are the result of the person's caregivers' unrealistic expectations.

Conflicting Discipline Reinforcement from Parents
In this case, one disciplinarian parent is dealing with a child strictly, while the other is extremely laid-back and encourages the child to take it easy far too often. Most children raised by such parents support the easygoing parent and regard the disciplinarian as a monster.

However, this develops into narcissism in the child, who becomes a spoiled brat under the "protection" of their easygoing parent.

Childhood Emotional Neglect
Many parents believe that if a child's physical needs are met, they will have a good life. As a result, they may make every effort to provide them with the best education, a decent home, and other necessities for their physical and mental development.

However, at the end of it all, a child feels emotionally uncared for and is vulnerable to narcissistic personality disorder.

Childhood Emotional Neglect (CEN) occurs when a caregiver ignores, minimizes, or dismisses a child's emotional life. Some even chastise or dismiss a child for being emotional. This deprives a child of appropriate affection, validation, attention, and emotional education, resulting in emotional immaturity or distortion.

Because they lack the necessary knowledge to deal with their unkempt emotions in a healthy manner, a child may develop defenses such as:

> ***Denial of Criticism***
> ***Overcompensation for their insecurities through an inflated ego.***
> ***They lack empathy because they did not learn it in the first place.***
> ***Manipulation tactics to satisfy their emotional needs***
> ***Attention-seeking behavior***

Comparative Motivation in Childhood

"Why don't you be like your friend James?"Why aren't you acting like other normal kids?" "You should be getting good grades as Dora!"

When parents compare their children to others in an attempt to motivate them, they are often unaware that they are harming the child's self-esteem. However, this is usually the case. And it promotes mental disorders such as narcissism, depression, and anxiety, among others. That's why it's classified as a comorbid psychological distress and life-threatening illness.

So, in an attempt to adapt to the comparisons, the child strives to be perfect, to be better than others, and develops chronic envy as they measure their success in terms of other children's success, as their parents' comparisons taught them.

Victim mentality

In the preceding influences, we have seen how the child's environment contributes to the development of the narcissistic mental health disorder. However, in this regard, the pathological narcissist contributes to their own misery because, regardless of the circumstances, you have the ability to choose how to react, whether negatively or positively.

If one adopts a victim mentality, narcissistic personality disorder will undoubtedly develop from adolescence to late adulthood.

This is not meant to be insensitive to the innocent child's plight, but rather to remind every narcissist that they do not have to be victims forever or use their childhood trauma as a justification for carrying on with this bad habit.

There is hope for change, no matter where you are in your understanding of narcissism.

Genetics

Pathological narcissism, like other personality disorders, is a product of both nature and nurture. While it is possible to grow up in an environment that promotes narcissism, some narcissists inherit these characteristics from their parents.

A recent behavioral genetic study, as well as other research on twins, confirm that narcissistic traits such as grandiosity and entitlement are slightly heritable. However, none demonstrate that it is entirely a genetic disorder.

Simply put, one may be genetically predisposed to developing narcissistic personality disorder (NPD), but risk factors such as unresolved emotional distress at a young age are required for the disorder to fully develop.

According to the American Psychiatric Association, narcissists are equally natured and nurtured, as both genetics and environment play a part. Some people are predisposed to developing a narcissistic personality disorder because they inherit certain characteristics, but risk factors such as poor parenting, childhood trauma, and victim mentality reinforce narcissistic personality traits.

Narcissistic personality disorder/NPD is typically diagnosed at the age of 18, but according to the Diagnostic and Statistical Manual of Mental Disorders, the underlying causes can be traced back to childhood.

Chapter 3

The Effect on Relationships

The consequences of narcissistic abuse can vary depending on how long someone can tolerate these types of relationships. The effects vary from mild to severe, with some survivors recovering while others suffering permanent damage. Here's how narcissistic abuse can affect a person's life.

Anxiety

Anxiety is common among narcissistic abuse survivors. Following narcissistic abuse, they may experience extreme fear or anxiety in new relationships. People who leave toxic relationships can develop separation anxiety, which causes them to feel panicked and disoriented when they are not with their abusers.

If they experience anxiety attacks, panic attacks, or hypervigilance after being abused by a narcissist, know that these symptoms will subside over time, especially if they can work through trauma with a professional.

Depression

Many people who have suffered narcissistic abuse develop depression. Survivors frequently experience feelings of inadequacy after months or years of being told how worthless and stupid they are by their abuser. Following years of manipulation and gaslighting, they may isolate themselves, exacerbating their depression.

Post-traumatic Stress

They will most likely exhibit symptoms of post-traumatic stress. Their minds will be on high alert, searching for danger. This is because the traumatic events elicited a fight or flight response from them. As a result, anything associated with those memories can elicit an anxiety response.

After experiencing narcissistic abuse, they may feel compelled to be on guard at all times. Victims of narcissism frequently mention that they never knew what their abuser would do next. They may find it difficult to relax as a result of chronic hypervigilance and anticipating the abuser around every corner.

They may also avoid situations or things that remind them of their abuse. This can range from avoiding specific places to avoiding specific people.

Loss of self and worth
They may feel like they've completely lost themselves. As a form of
brainwashing, narcissistic abuse can destroy a person's sense of self-worth.
They may no longer feel like the person they were before this happened.

Many people who have been subjected to narcissistic abuse find it difficult to
recognize themselves in the mirror because they no longer see their true
reflection.

They may also struggle to trust others, particularly those close to them, and
are constantly doubting or second-guessing themselves.

They may begin to believe that they are not good enough or that they caused
the abuse in the first place. This can lead to feelings of shame and
embarrassment, which may discourage them from seeking help.

They may also have difficulty making decisions. They may become perplexed
by simple decisions, or they may feel incapable of making any decisions at
all.

Narcissistic abusers frequently attempt to derail their own goals and
ambitions. They want complete control over everything about themselves,
including the activities that define who they are.

Inability to forgive themselves
Many victims of narcissistic abuse feel unworthy or believe they deserve how
the narcissist treated them. It may appear that there is something
fundamentally wrong with them if someone who is supposed to love them
unconditionally uses their power against them in such cruel ways. They may
have low self-esteem and believe that the narcissistic abuser would have
treated them better if they had behaved differently.

They may also have difficulty focusing on their goals and dreams. This could
be because they are still thinking about what happened to them. It's also
possible that their sense of self-worth has been so damaged that they can no
longer believe that anything good can happen in their lives.

Physical Symptoms
Physical symptoms, such as headaches, stomachaches, or body aches, may
persist after narcissistic abuse. After being subjected to narcissistic abuse,
they may struggle to sleep. They may be stressed about what happened and

unable to turn off their brain at night. Alternatively, they may experience
nightmares that linger for days.

Cognitive Problems

After narcissistic abuse, they may find it difficult to concentrate on daily tasks
such as finishing work or simply watching television. Traumatic memories are
known to interfere with concentration and focus. They may lose memory,
particularly in the short term. This is because trauma causes the brain to
release a surge of stress hormones, which affects the hippocampus region of
the brain.

Emotional Liability

After suffering from a traumatic event such as narcissistic abuse, it's not
uncommon to suffer sudden mood swings followed by irritability. Alternatively,
they may find themselves feeling emotionless and robotic. They may
experience depersonalization, which causes them to believe that everything
around them is inaccurate.

They may even feel the need to exact revenge on their abuser. However,
hatred for them only increases stress and anxiety, perpetuating mental health
issues.

Children's Reactions

If they have children who have witnessed narcissistic abuse, they may be
more likely to develop mental health issues like PTSD, anxiety disorders, or
depression. They may become fearful in situations that bring back memories
of their traumatic experiences. They might also have low self-esteem or
confidence issues, feel cut off from others, or be furious at the abuser or the
outside world.

Stuck in a cycle

Many people who have been victims of narcissistic abuse become trapped in
a cycle in which their abuser continues to contact them even after the
relationship has ended.

They may act nice, also known as hoovering, in an attempt to entice the
person back, make threats, or manipulate the person by making them feel
sorry for themselves. Narcissists may use this tactic to keep their victims
trapped in a cycle of abuse.

Problems with Trust

Following narcissistic abuse, their trust levels are likely to be extremely low. While this may appear to be a positive development, it may also have a negative impact on their future relationships. This issue could lead to other issues, such as social anxiety.

They may be constantly wondering whether people are telling them the truth or if they are simply manipulating their feelings to get what they want. They may become hyper-vigilant and overly sensitive to criticism or judgment from others as a result of their fear of being betrayed again.

They may have trust issues in all aspects of their life, such as personal relationships, friendships, work interactions, or even interaction with family members. They may also have insecure attachments, which means they are constantly concerned that people will abandon or betray them.

People Pleasing

They may become a people pleaser, attempting to make others like them. After walking on eggshells for so long, they may become overly accommodating in order to gain approval from others. They may struggle to express their emotions and thoughts following narcissistic abuse because they are afraid of being judged for what they say. They most likely suppressed their emotions to avoid confrontation with a narcissistic abuser.

Self-destructive habits

Narcissistic abuse can also lead to self-destructive behaviors. People who have been in relationships with narcissists may feel compelled to punish themselves because they believe they are to blame for their partner's bad behavior toward them.

They may struggle with addictions such as drinking, smoking, food addiction, or overspending. These addictions may be used to numb emotional pain.

Chapter 4

The Power of Self-Reflection

Self-awareness is the first step toward self-discovery, self-knowledge, and self-growth, as well as the key to feeling accomplished. However, I've recently begun to wonder how many of the tools that promote self-awareness also promote narcissism.

It's difficult to ignore the number of posts on social media that talk about how you should focus on yourself and set boundaries to protect yourself. Furthermore, it appears that everyone has been traumatized and must recover from it. This is a dangerous statement, and in my opinion, it can lead to misunderstandings and create trauma that did not exist in the first place.

Do not get me wrong. I am all about self-knowledge and self-awareness. When people embark on a journey of self-discovery, I believe it is an act of kindness because it genuinely helps them become better people. I wouldn't be here unless I believed in it.

But I also understand that happiness and contentment do not come from solitude. Because we are social creatures, we depend on one another. Focusing solely on your own goals and dreams will not provide you with satisfaction or a genuine sense of accomplishment. Narcissists and egoists are deeply unhappy and never satisfied. Nothing is sufficient for them. Contrary to popular belief, serving others brings happiness, according to Martin Seligman and his team's research. More specifically, the ability to use your skills to positively impact the lives of others will provide you with a sense of fulfillment.

Let's get into the nitty-gritty details of the tightrope we're walking when it comes to self- and leadership development, as well as how we can prevent narcissistic behavior.

Difference Between Self-awareness and Narcissism

The distinction between self-awareness and narcissism is in the purpose of the individual's focus on themselves. Self-awareness is the understanding of oneself, including one's strengths, weaknesses, and motivations. It entails reflecting inward to better understand how you can improve yourself and your relationships with others.

Narcissism, on the other hand, is a fixation on oneself that stems from self-admiration and a desire for admiration from others. It is an unhealthy preoccupation with oneself that frequently leads to manipulative or exploitative behaviors toward others.

Self-awareness, on the other hand, necessitates humility and an openness to being vulnerable. It entails acknowledging both your flaws and limitations, as well as your strengths and opportunities.

Narcissists lack humility; they are incapable of recognizing their own flaws and instead focus solely on their own greatness. They are also highly critical of those around them, despite having no real understanding of themselves or their behavior.

Ultimately, self-awareness leads to personal growth, whereas narcissism only feeds an inflated ego and exaggerates individual differences. Self-awareness enables you to recognize the impact you have on others and make changes to improve yourself and your relationships.

Narcissism, on the other hand, perpetuates selfishness and a sense of being entitled, which can lead to the dissolution of relationships with those around them. It is important to note that the narcissist will not be concerned about these broken relationships.

Understanding Self-awareness

When looking at the wellness industry, which promotes self-growth, it is clear that the coach's narcissistic tendencies imply that there is something wrong with you in the first place, but they, the coaches, are the ones who can fix you. There are empowerment coaches who claim to be able to make you feel empowered.

However, self-awareness is the authentic ability to understand how you affect and interact with others. It is your ability to understand what is going on inside you. That also implies that you have a healthy understanding of your emotions and do not overreact to every impulse you experience.

Cultivating self-awareness allows you to develop interpersonal skills, empathy, and emotional intelligence. You become more sensitive to the needs and perspectives of others, resulting in healthier and more satisfying relationships. Self-awareness also promotes personal growth and self-improvement by providing insights into your own behavior. This allows you to make intentional efforts to change and grow. It's a genuine insight journey that directs you outward. It is a necessary component for every leader.

Self-awareness in Everyday Life

At this point, you might point out that narcissism and self-awareness both require self-reflection and focus on oneself. However, self-awareness entails a balanced and objective understanding of oneself, whereas narcissism involves an exaggerated and self-aggrandizing perspective. Self-reflection by narcissists reinforces their inflated self-image rather than providing genuine insight. "Look how great I am" vs. "What do I excel at, and where do I need assistance?"

Self-awareness allows you to recognize your own strengths and weaknesses as you strive for personal development. Narcissists, on the other hand, frequently overestimate and distort their own worth. They frequently consider themselves superior to others and seek constant admiration.

The Narcissistic Component In Self-Development And Trauma Patience

Narcissism can emerge as a coping mechanism in response to trauma. People who have experienced trauma frequently feel overwhelmed by the emotions and feelings that accompany the experience, and they may develop a sense of detachment from their emotions as a coping mechanism. This detachment is what causes a lack of empathy for others, which is a defining feature of narcissism.

There is a delicate balance that must be recognized here, as excessive media focus on mental health can promote the development of trauma and, as a result, narcissism. This occurs when a person focuses solely on posts that encourage self-focus without compassion or without contextualizing the post in the context of our interconnectedness.

Narcissists, no matter how much they appear to love themselves, are constantly seeking praise or admiration. They crave validation from others and frequently brag or exaggerate their accomplishments in order to gain recognition. They also enjoy feeling appreciated, which boosts their ego. This behavior is extrinsically centered, as the narcissist is concerned with eliciting an external reaction, as opposed to internally focused self-awareness, which focuses on improving relationships and living with intention. It is the distinction between "How can I improve myself to serve others" and "How can I make others see me as unique".

Self-development, like everything else in the world, is a practice of balance. Too much of it does lead to the emergence of narcissistic traits, and in a world of social media, it is our responsibility to use our ability to be self-aware of how we are affecting our environment. Remember, there is no "I" without "Us," which is why self-awareness is more than just how to improve your own life. Making a better life for yourself inherently implies cultivating better relationships and, as a result, playing a far more positive role.

Chapter 5

Building Empathy and Compassion

Empathy is an important component of healthy relationships, but people with narcissistic traits may struggle to understand and express emotions other than their own. However, empathy exists on a spectrum, and you can develop empathy with practice and effort. Here are some practical strategies for developing empathy:

Focus on developing positive relationships
Invest your time and energy in making meaningful connections with others. Real people are interested in developing those relationships, and they take the time to demonstrate that they care. Making connections and forming healthier relationships is at the heart of empathetic behavior.

Search for common ground
Discover shared experiences or passions to connect with others and develop empathy. Make a list of common interests you share with the most important people in your life. The more you realize you have more in common than what divides you, the better your relationship will be and the more empathetic you will be towards them.

Avoid criticism and judgment
Keep in mind that every person has a different viewpoint and background. A sensitive person does not judge because they do not wish to be judged. This is also true for someone with pathological narcissism. They have typically been judged sufficiently, which is part of the problem. So it's past time to put a stop to this type of bad behavior. It has already caused enough damage.

Practice patience
Give people the time and room they need to talk about themselves and their experiences. Even though you're interested in saying something, it's simple to get into a habit of responding automatically. Rather, listen intently to what they have to say, hearing as though you can trust every word.

Develop your emotional vocabulary

Try to identify the emotions you're experiencing and understand how they affect your own behavior and interactions with others. Make a list of emotions you've experienced and how they make you react to practice this.

Effect of your actions on others

Be mindful of how you treat others and how your actions impact their emotions and well-being. Once you understand your own emotions and how they affect your behavior, you can better understand how your behavior may affect the emotions and behavior of others. You know what it does to you; now imagine what it does to others.

Practice empathy for yourself

Recognize and validate your own emotions and needs, and then show the same level of understanding and empathy to others. Empathy for yourself can help you extend the same courtesy to others. This, believe it or not, maybe the most difficult thing for people suffering from pathological narcissism to do.

You've most likely spent your entire life judging yourself more harshly than you do others. Practice saying nice things to yourself at least three times per day. The more you care about yourself, the more you will develop empathy for others.

Practice active listening

Pay attention to what the other person is saying, ask clarifying questions, and respond with empathetic behavior such as offering a hug or simply displaying sensitive body language. Try out a few different empathetic responses for this type of exercise.

Concentrate on understanding the emotions of others

Pay attention to their body language and tone of voice to gain insight into their emotions. Mirroring emotions through nonverbal cues such as body language and compassionate facial expressions is part of the affective experience.

Use I-statements instead of blame language

Concentrate on expressing your own emotions and needs without criticizing the other person. Nobody makes you feel any specific way. Nobody can make you happy or sad; only you have control over your emotions. Instead of saying, "You make me feel...," say, "I feel (sad, happy, depressed, etc.) when you (do this). That is an example of you taking responsibility for your own emotions, so there is no need to attack others when you are feeling bad.

Avoid interrupting others

Allow them to finish speaking before you respond. Sometimes you think they're going to say something they didn't intend to say. So you'll have to wait until they're done to get the full story. They will believe you are genuinely interested, and you will have more information to formulate a more appropriate response.

Practice accepting and validating

Recognize and accept the other person's feelings, even if you disagree with them. This is a difficult one, but it is critical to generating more empathy. Try to understand why they feel the way they do, and you will be able to express that their feelings are valid, even if you disagree.

When necessary, apologize

Accept accountability for your deeds and offer your regrets. For someone with pathological narcissism, this is challenging, but it's essential to learning empathy. Sensitive people need to acknowledge when they have harmed others and take appropriate action to make things right.

Practice expressing gratitude

Show appreciation for others' efforts and contributions. It is also beneficial for you to simply recognize the positive things and people in your daily life. This can help you feel more compassionate toward those around you, as well as improve your overall mood.

Be mindful of nonverbal clues

Consider how your actions and body language may influence others. Use open body language to express your interest and concern about what they're saying. Avoid crossing your arms and maintain eye contact to make them feel heard. This will allow you to better understand their feelings.

Imagine yourself in someone else's shoes

Try to understand things from their perspective. Try to fully imagine how you'd feel in that situation. Keep a journal of your observations. This will help you develop both cognitive and affective empathy, as well as strengthen your overall empathy capacity.

Try to put aside your feelings—or lack thereof—and consider what the other person might be going through. Even those who suffer from pathological narcissism can empathize with others. Think about how you would feel based on that. You two may be able to connect more as a result of this.

By adopting these empathy strategies into your daily conversations, you can boost your emotional intelligence and form deeper, more meaningful connections with those around you. Developing empathy is a critical skill for building strong relationships, and while it can be difficult for people with pathological narcissism, it is not impossible. You can improve your empathy skills and enjoy healthier, happier relationships as a result.

Chapter 6

Developing Healthy Relationships

Understanding your narcissistic tendencies and their impact on your partner can be difficult, but it is critical to building a healthier relationship. Begin by identifying patterns in your behavior, such as a need to be in control or ignoring your partner's emotions. Recognizing these behaviors and their negative effects on your partner can be a critical step toward overcoming narcissism.

It is also critical to recognize your partner's narcissistic tendencies. This can manifest itself in a variety of ways, including constantly seeking attention and admiration, belittling or criticizing others, and refusing to accept responsibility for his or her actions. If you feel like you're constantly stepping on your partner's toes or that their needs aren't being met, it could be an indication of narcissistic behavior.

Ignoring or discounting narcissistic behavior in a relationship can lead to emotional abuse and long-term mental health problems. Going to therapy or counseling can be an effective way to resolve these issues and improve the overall health of the relationship.

Narcissistic behavior not only harms the narcissist's partner, but it can also harm the narcissist himself or herself. Feelings of superiority and a lack of empathy can result in loneliness, isolation, and difficulty making genuine connections with others. Recognizing the harm that narcissism can cause you and your partner can motivate you to take action.

In addition, narcissism can cause a lack of self-awareness and an inability to accept responsibility for your actions. This can lead to conflict and misunderstandings in the relationship, as the narcissist may refuse to admit their mistakes or apologize for their behavior. It is critical that both partners communicate openly and honestly about their feelings and concerns, and that the narcissist work to develop empathy and self-reflection skills in order to improve the relationship.

It can be hard to recognize your narcissism, but there are some indicators to look out for. Do you often prioritize your own needs and desires over those of your partner? Do you seek validation from others, or do you feel entitled? Do you have difficulty empathizing with your partner or seeing things from their perspective? Answering these questions honestly can assist you in recognizing narcissistic tendencies in your behavior.

Another indicator of narcissism in a relationship is a lack of accountability. Do you blame your partner for relationship problems, rather than accepting responsibility for your own actions? Do you make excuses for your actions or refuse to apologize when you hurt your partner? This could be an early sign of narcissistic behavior.

It's important to remember that everyone has some degree of narcissism, but it becomes a problem when it starts to harm relationships. If you suspect you have narcissistic tendencies, you should seek help from a therapist or counselor. They can assist you in overcoming these narcissistic behaviors and developing healthier ways of interacting with others.

Steps to Improve Your Relationship

Once you've identified your narcissistic tendencies and understand how they affect your relationship, you can take steps to effectively manage them. As previously stated, increasing self-awareness, empathy, and emotional regulation can be effective tools for reducing narcissistic behavior.

It is critical that you discuss your narcissistic issues with your partner honestly and openly. This can help you better understand their behavior and provide support for improving your relationship. Going to therapy or counseling may also help you address underlying issues and develop healthy coping mechanisms.

As discussed in the previous chapter, one of the most important aspects of overcoming narcissism is cultivating self-awareness and empathy. By being able to recognize your own emotions, thoughts, and behaviors without passing judgment on them, you can identify patterns in your behavior and take deliberate action to change them. Developing empathy and focusing on your partner's needs and feelings can also help build a happier and more balanced relationship.

Another significant component of developing self-awareness is seeking feedback from others. Narcissists often find it difficult to accept criticism or feedback, but it is critical to listen to and consider other people's points of view. This can help you understand how your actions affect those around you and identify areas for improvement.

It's also important to practice self-care. Narcissists frequently prioritize their own needs over those of others, but ignoring self-care can lead to burnout and put additional strain on relationships. Taking time for oneself, participating in activities that bring us joy, and seeking support from loved ones can all help us live a healthier, more balanced life.

Managing one's emotions can be an important step in avoiding harmful behavior toward one's partner. Mindfulness, meditation, and journaling are all techniques that can help you become more aware of your emotions and practice healthy emotional regulation. Learning to identify triggers can also help you avoid negative behaviors.

Deep breathing exercises are another technique for regulating emotions. When you're stressed or overwhelmed, take a deep breath for several seconds to help relax your body and mind. To help you decompress and feel better, try engaging in physical activities such as yoga or exercise. Seeing a therapist or counselor can also help you learn techniques and tools to improve your emotional control and relationships.

Narcissism frequently leads to a lack of active listening skills and poor communication. Practicing effective communication skills, such as using "I" statements and active listening strategies, can help you build trust and foster more productive conversations. These abilities can also help you validate your partner's experiences and express your own feelings.

Avoiding assumptions is another important strategy for improving your listening and communication skills. It's common to assume we know how our partner feels or thinks, but doing so can lead to miscommunication and resentment. Alternatively, use open-ended questions to encourage your partner to share their feelings and thoughts with you. This can strengthen your relationship and allow you to better understand their point of view.

If your narcissism has damaged your relationship, it may take some time and effort to rebuild trust and mend it. Express sincere regret and accept responsibility for your actions. Pay close attention and make an effort to understand what your partner says. Positive and consistent behavior can help to regain trust over time.

It is critical to recognize that regaining trust following narcissistic behavior is a continuous process. It is critical to be patient and understanding with your partner as he or she works through his or her feelings and emotions. It is also critical to seek professional assistance, such as therapy, to address any underlying issues that may be contributing to their narcissistic behavior. You can work toward a healthier and stronger relationship with your partner by following these steps.

It is important to remember that seeking professional help does not imply that you are weak or defective. Admitting that you need help and taking the first steps toward your development requires bravery and self-awareness. A licensed therapist or counselor can help you identify the root causes of your narcissistic tendencies and work with you to develop more positive coping strategies and effective communication techniques. With the right help, you can overcome narcissism and develop stronger, more fulfilling relationships.

Overcoming narcissism in a relationship is a difficult yet rewarding process. With dedication and effort, you can change your behavior and cultivate a more harmonious, balanced relationship. You can create a relationship based on love and respect for one another rather than egotistical behavior by emphasizing self-awareness, empathy, and constructive communication.

Active listening is an important step toward maintaining a healthy and balanced relationship. This entails truly listening to and understanding your partner's point of view, without interrupting or ignoring their emotions. By actively listening, you increase trust and enhance your emotional connection.

Establishing boundaries is yet another crucial component of preserving a happy partnership. It is critical to clearly communicate your needs and expectations while also respecting your partner's boundaries. This can help to avoid conflict and lay the groundwork for mutual respect and understanding.

Chapter 7

Seeking Professional Help

Experts believe that therapy is the most effective treatment for narcissistic personality disorder. Therapy for Narcissistic Personality Disorder (NPD) can help individuals become more aware of their narcissistic tendencies and their impact on others. Additionally, it can help them begin to understand and control their emotions.

Low empathy is a common symptom of narcissistic personality disorder, but research shows that empathy can be learned. Therapy can help people with NPD learn to accept responsibility for their actions and thus build healthier relationships. Therapy is necessary because it can address more than just the symptoms of narcissistic personality disorder. It can concentrate on treating comorbid symptoms and mental health conditions like bipolar disorder and other personality disorders that frequently coexist with NPD.

Therapy will not be able to overnight transform someone who presents as "narcissistic. Years may pass before numerous individuals see any real progress. However, if they are eager to work on their narcissistic tendencies and dedicate themselves to therapy, even if NPD cannot be cured, treatment can be extremely beneficial.

Therapy can help with traits, but narcissism cannot be treated on its own. The mindful space of therapy is an excellent place to reflect on any insecurities or self-esteem issues that may be at the root of it. A professional clinician can provide the necessary support to establish more realistic expectations and address how a person's behavior may impact their relationships.

Treatment Options for NPD

Narcissistic personality disorder can be difficult to treat and takes time to develop. This is why it is critical to find the best type of therapy for narcissistic personality disorder based on each person's unique requirements. The first step is becoming aware of the various types of therapy.

DBT stands for Dialectical Behavior Therapy

Dialectical behavioral therapy, a subtype of cognitive behavioral therapy, helps patients improve their ability to manage their emotions, form relationships, and cope with stress. Although DBT was originally developed to treat borderline personality disorder, we have discovered that it is also an effective treatment for narcissistic personality disorder. It usually includes both individual and group therapy sessions.

EMDR therapy (Eye Movement Desensitisation and Reprocessing)
Research suggests that early childhood trauma and NPD may be linked. EMDR therapy assists people in processing and compartmentalizing trauma, which is likely why it may be useful in the treatment of NPD. EMDR therapy requires patients to perform guided eye movements while discussing traumatic or negative events with their therapist. This could eventually alleviate the distressing effects of these traumatic events.

Metacognitive Interpersonal Therapy (MIT)
Although people with NPD may exhibit similar traits and behaviors, the disease does not affect everyone in the same way. Experts believe that there are several types of narcissistic personality disorder. These subtypes can change how NPD affects a person's daily life.

An example of this would be the grandiose subtype, which may cause individuals to exhibit more outward displays of wrath and aggression. On the other hand, a person who possesses the vulnerable subtype is more likely to be fragile when confronted with criticism and may also suffer from low expectations of themselves.

Psychotherapy
Psychotherapy, often known as talk therapy, consists of continual one-on-one conversations between the patient and the counselor. Participating in individual therapy sessions gives individuals the opportunity to talk about their emotions and behaviors with a healthcare expert. Through the process of being conscious of what they are doing, they will eventually be able to learn how to manage their thoughts and behaviors.

Cognitive Behavioral Treatment (CBT)
It is possible for people to recognize harmful or unhelpful thought patterns with the assistance of cognitive-behavioral therapy. Once an individual is aware of these patterns, they are able to take action to alter them from their current state. People who are having cognitive behavioral therapy (CBT) treatment are frequently given homework to complete in between sessions. This is in addition to the practice of skills with a caregiver.

Transference Focused Psychotherapy (TFP)

This is a highly structured style of psychotherapy in which patients are urged to express their sentiments toward a specific person, experience, or scenario to their caregiver. This allows individuals to process their feelings in a secure, regulated, and directed atmosphere. It can help people begin to adjust their views toward themselves and others.

Mindfulness-Based Therapy (MBT)

Mentalization-based treatment encourages people to reflect on their real thought processes or the way they think. Its objective is to help people see the connections between their thoughts and behaviors. DBT can also assist people in better comprehending those around them, which can be difficult for anyone with NPD.

Gestalt Therapy

A style of psychotherapy that stresses the present rather than the past. Therapy sessions are often focused on the issues the individual is currently facing in life. Role-playing social interactions is a typical activity in Gestalt therapy to aid patients with their conflict-resolution strategies.

Schema Therapy

Schema therapy combines components of psychotherapy and cognitive behavioral therapy to aid people in discovering and modifying their internal patterns of learned ideas and actions. Many persons with NPD acquire maladaptive schemas at a young age. Individuals can seek to change their habits once they are detected.

When identifying the optimal sort of therapy for NPD, it is crucial to examine symptoms and aims. For example, EMDR may be an incredibly successful kind of treatment for someone dealing with previous trauma, whereas someone who has not experienced trauma may benefit more from present-focused therapy, such as Gestalt therapy.

Learning more about narcissistic personality disorder therapy enables you to select the most appropriate type of therapy for your specific symptoms, requirements, and goals. You can think about the goals you want to achieve and then choose the therapeutic technique that will best help you.

Narcissistic personality disorder is a highly complex syndrome that impacts how people perceive themselves and others. It can be a tough mental disease to treat, so only seek therapy with an experienced practitioner.

As you can see, there are many different techniques for treating narcissistic personality disorder in therapy. Although persons with NPD are frequently hesitant to seek treatment, therapy can help them focus on the detrimental behaviors and symptoms that influence them in their daily lives.

You can now receive the assistance you require to cope with NPD in the privacy of your own home, for as long as it is convenient for you. You do not have to tolerate the unpleasant parts of NPD. You can learn to handle it.

Chapter 8

Embracing vulnerability

Expressing our whole truths can be tough in any situation, but it appears that men's interactions with emotions are especially strained. Why is it so difficult for males to be vulnerable? Perhaps it is as simple as searching up the dictionary definition of the word: "capable of or susceptible to being attacked, damaged, or hurt."

Many of us were educated to believe that vulnerability is terrible and a weakness, but putting up a solid barrier is good and macho. While there has been an increase in conversation concerning these stereotypes and limiting attitudes, little progress has been made, with vulnerability widely accepted among men. The expectation to be "macho" remains the prevalent and accepted behavioral method for embodying the cis-gendered concept of manhood. Anything less can call into question one's "man card".

When we analyze why males struggle with vulnerability, the primary cause appears to be fear. This dread takes numerous forms, including the fear of being wounded, damaged, or ridiculed. Although vulnerability may seem to indicate leaving oneself exposed to assault, in actuality, it can be the path to mental fortitude and power. When we let down our boundaries, even just a little, we allow ourselves to experience a greater spectrum of emotions and experiences, both individually and collectively. Being vulnerable allows us to better understand ourselves while also cultivating and deepening our relationships with others. It can also help us better grasp our potential for development, raise our self-awareness, and strengthen our emotional intelligence.

Benefits of Vulnerability

Enhances mental wellness
Suppressing our feelings and emotions is a losing proposition. This approach not only fails miserably in dealing with our emotions, but it is also short-lived. Those emotions and feelings may appear to be dormant, but they frequently reemerge at the most inconvenient times, causing us to erupt, albeit accidentally. This eruption has the potential to have both short- and long-term negative consequences. A healthier approach to this issue is to acknowledge,

experience, express, and then release our emotions so that they do not accumulate to the point where they harm us and those who are close to us without warning. This approach is supported by science, including a brain study by UCLA psychologists that discovered that verbally expressing our emotions reduces the intensity of sadness, anger, and pain. It's hard to believe that simply speaking one's truth can help soothe and heal some of the most difficult emotions we face as humans. Instead of allowing emotions to be suppressed, try using the power of vulnerability to cope with emotions in the moment while also strengthening your mental health over time.

Improves relationships
Regardless of whether we acknowledge it, we all have emotional needs in our relationships. When they are not met, it leads to mistrust and resentment. Numerous studies have confirmed what many of us already know anecdotally: we all have different emotional needs, with some preferring emotional connection over physical connection and others needing physical connection before feeling an emotional tie. Men can help meet their emotional needs by being vulnerable with potential or current partners. Aside from intimate partners, displaying vulnerability is an excellent way to establish trust with anyone in your life. If you are willing to be open, transparent, and even put yourself "at risk," you send a clear message to the other person that you trust them with the most intimate parts of yourself. This simple act lays the groundwork for a long-term relationship, whether romantic or not.

Aids in breaking the cycle
Many societies today are dealing with an acute epidemic that is afflicting young men. Many children are raised with toxic attitudes and faulty beliefs, which often lead to adults who inadvertently, and sometimes intentionally, harm others. Repressed feelings accumulate over time, much like a pressure cooker. Toxic masculinity has been linked in numerous studies to sexual violence, traffic accidents, road rage, harassment, violence, alcoholism, depression, and even suicide. Those are exorbitant prices to "pay" to avoid the perceived risk of connecting with oneself and sharing difficult emotions with a trustworthy source. The irony of the fear of appearing weak is that vulnerability is linked to higher levels of self-confidence rather than lower levels. We want young people to see vulnerability as a strength, not a weakness. To do so, however, we must first remove the stigma associated with feeling and expressing emotion. In other words, men will need to reshape our widely held attitudes and beliefs about the opposition to not only discussing but also feeling our emotions. We must learn to accept that being human is imperfect and, while vulnerable, it does not undermine our masculinity. Introducing vulnerability into the mix could be the key to helping

us move away from this unhealthy behavior and toward raising well-rounded, stable, and healthy young people.

Shifting perspectives and unlearning the long and deep history of taboos surrounding vulnerability and masculinity requires a significant amount of time, energy, patience, and openness. Too often, it takes hitting rock bottom or, at the very least, a brick wall to cause a change in perspective. Even then, it may not work. However, when we acknowledge our emotions, the rewards are rich, deep, and long-lasting, giving us the freedom to grow, cultivate more meaningful relationships, and create our own definitions of who we can be more fully. Accepting vulnerability and being your true self enables you to:

> *Develop a stronger sense of identity, allowing you to be true to yourself.*
> *Be more focused, and allow yourself and others to make mistakes.*
> *Concentrate on self-investment and personal development.*
> *Accept yourself and be who you truly are, rather than who you believe you should be.*

Ways to practice being vulnerable

Train your awareness to catch yourself when you say something harsh or restricting to yourself. Nothing that you wouldn't say to someone else should be said to yourself, for example, would you tell someone in your life to "man up" when they face a difficult situation? Would you tell someone else they "should" act in this or that way? Try treating yourself with grace and openness to whatever feels right for you.

Check out the wellness wheel. It can be beneficial to delve deeper into what aspects of ourselves we may be overlooking and how we can better nurture those areas of our lives. Do you require assistance in expressing your emotions? You can also practice telling the truth by using emotions and examples from The Feelings Wheel. If you're up for it, both of these explorations could be used to delve deeper into vulnerability through journaling!

Consider speaking with a trusted loved one, a behavioral health coach, or a therapist to begin practicing and flexing your vulnerable muscles. Like any learned skill, this can be difficult at first but becomes easier with practice.

Conclusion

It can be difficult for a narcissist to recognize their own traumas. However, if you feel as if you are always carrying a heavy burden, your trauma requires attention in order to heal. To deal with your narcissistic tendencies, try forgiving yourself for past mistakes, building your self-esteem, and reflecting on your defense mechanisms. Overcoming narcissism begins with you, which may require time and dedication. Take one day at a time, please. Along with much more, these are the main conclusions:

Consider the reasons behind your actions
Although your reactions may come unexpectedly, your body sends you signals before they happen. Pay attention to all of your body's signals after a stressful event. Examine the reasons for your behavior. Are there any patterns in your actions? Did you get angry because of something someone said or did? This can help you understand your narcissistic tendencies.

Pause before reacting
It may appear that you go from 0 to 60 in a split second. When you are triggered, though, take a deep breath and pause before reacting. Leave the situation until you have regained your composure. Once you've mastered this process, you can wait even longer for the rational part of your brain to "switch back on". Reacting out of shame will not help you in the long run.

Determine an alternative reaction
When things don't go as planned, consider different ways to express your anger or frustration. Could you respond with grace or silence rather than anger? Determine what reaction you would have and practice it mentally. This can help you perform better in future stressful situations or interactions.

Pay attention to how others feel
You may need to examine your relationships if you want to stop being a narcissist. Narcissists frequently focus on themselves, making it impossible for them to support others. A relationship is a two-way street, and other people's feelings matter. Take a break and remember that your partner's feelings and views are equally important. Consider asking a friend or family member how they're doing and paying close attention to their response.

Accept that others aren't perfect
Recognize that no one is perfect, including those closest to you, such as parents, friends, and caregivers. If you have narcissistic tendencies, you may feel a strong desire to control your environment. Letting go of the fact that

everyone is unique and will inevitably make mistakes reduces stress and allows you to be more accepting of the way things stand.

Remember your value

Remember that your worth is intrinsic and not based on your perfection. NPD is frequently accompanied by an underlying theme of shame, which can lead to other harmful behaviors, such as lashing out when feelings of worthlessness arise. These are the moments when you need to remind yourself that your worth does not depend on perfection.

Forgive yourself

Forgive yourself for creating unrealistic expectations and consider why you set them so high. Instead of beating yourself up when you don't meet your goals, accept responsibility for your actions. You are human and will make mistakes, so allow yourself to feel compassion for them.

Let yourself feel your emotions

Allow yourself to experience emotions rather than attempting to control every outcome. Even the unpleasant feelings we have provide us with information. If you ignore or suppress your emotions, they will eventually reveal themselves, usually in explosive and destructive ways.

Managing Stress

Use stress management techniques to overcome avoidance behaviors.6 It may appear easier to react angrily to stress if this is your habitual behavior. Stress management is extremely beneficial when trying to become less narcissistic. These techniques can help you recognize triggers, develop healthy coping mechanisms, and reduce outbursts and negative behaviors.

Meditation

Meditate to process emotions in a different way, allowing yourself to be present and notice thoughts or feelings. You can't "fix" narcissism, but meditation helps you to sit back and think about your tendencies. Meditation can take many forms and does not have to involve sitting in silence for an extended period of time.

You can find a method that works for you by consulting a professional or following a guided meditation session. You may feel insecure and vulnerable at first, so begin gradually and adjust your routine as needed.

Take one day at a time

Remember that you cannot control the outcome of every future situation. When we are concerned about what will happen tomorrow or the next day, we become more anxious. We imagine stressful scenarios that may or may not occur. This increases stress and anger, especially if things turn out differently than we expected. Taking things one day at a time can help to alleviate the need to control everything. Concentrate on what you can change.

Explore a new hobby

Cultivate self-love and express yourself through art forms such as painting, writing, music, or dance. Finding a fresh pastime is a healthy distraction and a way to channel your energy into something productive and positive. Rather than reacting to stress or anxiety with anger or rage, take a moment to engage your creative side.

Identify your triggers

We never know what will set us off, so it's critical to recognize the early warning signs of anger. To learn how not to be a narcissist, you must be prepared for angry outbursts. One of the first steps toward healing is to identify your triggers.

Pay attention to when you become angry or need to control a situation. What was happening at the time? What caused your frustration? The answers will provide clues about what triggers you, allowing you to be more proactive in the future. You will be able to cope with difficult emotions and stop hurting those around you in this way.

Spend time in nature.

Spending time in nature can help to reduce anxiety, narcissistic depression, stress, and other mental health issues. The outdoors provides an opportunity to access and reflect on feelings of happiness and joy, and nature is readily available. Being in nature improves mental health, so spending just a few minutes outside connecting with the earth can have a significant impact on your mood.

Start apologizing

Apologizing includes admitting your error and putting yourself in a vulnerable situation. You may respond to vulnerability with narcissistic wrath or rage. Remember that everyone makes errors. Admitting them promotes trust with people, sustains connections, and provides authenticity.

Do good for others
Giving support is equally as beneficial as receiving it. By doing something pleasant for others, you can encourage and cheer them on. This displays that you care about them and that it is not simply about you and your needs.

Maximizing people's potential
It's easy to believe that individuals are untrustworthy, unpleasant, or trying to take advantage of you. But these are only concepts, not facts. If you distrust others, alter your thinking to a more caring one. You may not know the complete story behind someone's actions. It is possible that they did not aim to damage you. This can help you regulate your reactions and mood.

Learn to listen
Don't interrupt or redirect a conversation to make it completely yours. Being a good friend, family member, or spouse includes listening to and supporting individuals in your group. Active listening means not interrupting. You listen to what they're saying and allow them room to express themselves.

Practice self-love
Remember to be gentle with yourself, providing grace on difficult days. If you continue to engage in unhealthy routines, such as beating yourself up or condemning yourself for being vulnerable, your behavior will not change. We are all flawed and deserve unfailing love. Self-love practice can assist you in mending your emotional traumas and cultivating compassion for the world around you.

Begin writing a diary
Keep a record of your thoughts, feelings, and where they originate from. Read them aloud to yourself. This may make you feel vulnerable, yet expressing your feelings on paper can be revealing. A diary is also a great tool for recognizing your thought patterns and how they affect your mood and function. If reading a diary feels too heavy for you, start with a shorter term or combine it with another habit to retain consistency.

Many people with NPD make every effort to make every environment favorable to mindfulness. This can be a difficult habit to change, but focusing on it communicates to everyone around you that you are adjusting your behavior and realizing that you are not the most important person in the room.